A PAINTING OF SAND

Poems from Ghost Ranch

L. Luis López

For Theresa / con mucho cariño / L. Luis López / 11/15/200

Farolito Press
Grand Junction, Colorado

ISBN 0-9679844-1-6
Library of Congress Catalog Card No. 00-132305

Cover by Andrew Gruner

Farolito Press
P.O. Box 60003
Grand Junction, Colorado 81506

For Ghost Ranch

Table of Contents

INTRODUCTION

These poems are inspired by a number of visits and stays at Ghost Ranch near Abiquiu, New Mexico. This is a high desert area. The beauty and the atmosphere of this area during any season of the year has a special quality that inspires writers, artists, and anyone with spiritual interests (in the broad sense of that term). The lead poem, "Abiquiu," is also the final poem in this collection. It captures what Ghost Ranch means to me, and after a reading of the poems and perhaps after your own experiences at Ghost Ranch, I hope the final reading of "Abiquiu" will capture your own feelings about this high desert area.

L. Luis López

ABIQUIU

Take this city-filled
soul,
pour it out,
place it in soil
beneath
your high desert vista.

Fill it with canyon,
sky,
mesa,
mountain,
smell of rain,
and
song of bird.

Tint each
with time of day.

Let each
settle
into a painting of sand

so that when I'm away
I can
close my eyes
and gaze upon
and breathe your sacred strands.

BIRD

At gray of dawn
it sits
atop
a scrub of pine

Its open throat
pours
forth the sound of its soul

Dark

As the sun rises
dark
seems to shrink
then hide
beneath a pebble

As the sun sets
it peeks
then spreads forth serenely

CHIMNEY ROCK

Hot, cold, wind, and water
have
Oh! So intricately carved you.

How I wish with me time
had
been so kind.

KITCHEN MESA

At sunset a table
Set
With
Colorful cloud

Orange and Watermelon

DUST DEVIL

I watch
the
wind partner
the dust

Embraced they whirl
as one
across the desert floor

RAIN

finally
an
afternoon shower

this evening
rainbow
skies

rainbow
hills tomorrow

ABIQUIU RESERVOIR

beyond the highway
among the dry
hills
sits a lake

changing gem
set
in sand and granite shades

a
compliment
to
engineer jewelers

but many mourn
nature
and
a people's
history
lost
or hidden
within
the gem's expanse

puddle by the library

rain drops form
air
domes
on the puddle's surface

they sail here and there
sometimes
merging
into doubles or clusters

futuristic water craft
I think

o o

                               o

              oo   oOo

                     oo

O

       o

plink! plink! plink! POP!

afternoon cloud

your shadow
weaves
over
hill over
hill over hill over hill

desert shower

summer thunder
threatens
then
releases
a half-hearted shower

enough

to set a flower fire

day hike

at noon
I count
nine evergreens
along
the cliff's edge

coiled trunks
twisting

no
motion

toward the sun

why am I in such a hurry?

night storm

even if seconds

apart

each time jagged bolts
rip
across
the black sky

exposing
a swirl of ragged cloud

exposing
our
upturned frightened
faces

necks and shoulders
cringing
to turbulent thunder

it is unexpected

after the night storm

blue and pink
blossom
sporadic
noiseless
on the distant horizon

HUMMINGBIRD FLOWERS
(Indian Paintbrush)

the yellow sand radiates heat so dry

I wonder how
cactus, grass, and shrub survive

noon heat so intense

I wonder how
anything can crawl, or walk, or fly

yet a crimson paintbrush attracts

a purple-green blur
with beak that feeds on nectar

composed, I'm told, through roots

that feed on neighbor roots
and all the more

I wonder how
cactus, grass, and shrub survive

RIO CHAMA

in October you
wind
so slow
around each boulder

your
gentle belly
brushing
bedded pebbles

in June you
drive you
whirl
in spuming fury
at the boulders
and
unable
to budge them

roughly
unbed
the polished pebbles

hawk

your flight leaves
no track
in sky
by
which I can retrace you
but
soar, slant, and skim
somehow
help
me to remember

box canyon

your
walls
tower
to the sky,
but
lean back
on me
as
I
look up

CANE CHOLLA
(during a lightning storm)

sitting cross legged in the dark
of my tent
I look out at the gathering storm

clicks of lightning illuminate
the air
around between arms and stalk

each time a skeleton

CANE CHOLLA
(during a full moon)

sitting cross legged in the dark
of my tent
I look out at the light of the moon

it washes the night with soft light
bathes
each branch with ghostly aura

all night a saint

CANE CHOLLA
(during morning sunlight)

sitting cross legged in the early light
of my tent
I wait for the warmth of the sun

a strong shaft of light streams
through the pines
emblazons a thousand silver thorns

for the moment a treasure tree

ANTS

The patch of ground at my feet
teems with red ants,
black ants,
piss ants.
All pattern
this space by the thousands
with no lengthy
direction-three lengths
this way, five that, ten back,
sudden crisscross,
barely
missing,
and when two meet,
click apart
like two magnets-
stunned
for a micro second,
each recovers-continues on.

Some kind of beetle, twice
the size of
the largest ant,
works a determined path
across the pattern,
meets an ant,
pops
ten lengths size
into the air,
falls, rights itself-continues on.

CERRO PEDERNAL

the mountain rises dark
into the storm

fire sparks from rim
to base
from base to rim

sounds of anger-deep-shrill
drive dust and rain
across
the valley grass
ahead
it seems of worse to come

the mountain is the source
I think
but as I look

a shaft of light through cloud
reveals a miracle
of green
on western slope
that travels
north
along its base
across
the valley grass towards me

for awhile now
the mountain
and I
are bathed in yellow calm

sounds of anger forgotten

SNAKEWEED

"Escoba de culebra" the ranch guide
said
as he pointed at the snakeweed
"and some people
use it as a broom even today"

that explained "escoba"
but I didn't
think
to ask about "culebra"
so here I am in the Ghost Ranch
library
wondering
about "culebra"
snake
at ten o'clock at night

under Snakeweed one book
reads
Gutierrezia sarothrae,
sarothrae
meaning of the broom in Latin
from the Greek
sarotan

Gutierrezia for Pedro Gutierrez
botanist
from Madrid

another book adds
under Broom Snakeweed
Microcephalia
Greek for many tiny heads

one other
points out the flowers are
of the Sunflower Family

and
the Museum Trail Guide

says
it blooms here in the Fall
toxic
to cattle

so when it yellows the entire llano
the ranchero
understands overgrazing

another book
lists
Snakeweed under Matchbrush

Whew!

in all this highfalutin
and
not so highfalutin
naming
nothing explains "culebra"
snake
and
I bet nothing will explain "match"

tomorrow I'll just have to ask

Oh

weed and brush I understand

Bugs in the Campground in June

I think that flying bug thinks
my sunburned ear
is a flower
the way
it buzzes and tries to enter

Ear wax, my friend, is
all you'll get
and
what you get
will not produce another me
if
you enter someone else's ear

PRICKLY PEAR

Sunday morning
the prickly pear
flowers
a sun,
yellow petals
cupping
a broad ring of red,
a ring of yellow,
ring of green,
the very center black.

A bee of green visits
the sun,
brushes the center
in lazy buzz,
feeds
at nectar glands
then carries
particles
of life to other suns.

Monday morning
I notice
this sun has closed
its petals.

NEEDLE-AND-THREAD GRASS

When the needle-and-thread grass
begins to curl,
you must look closely.
It's communicating in cursive-
Y, n, g, q, i, l, l, w, o, c, b, d, f, e-
every letter of the alphabet.
If you stand there long enough
and vary your angle,
I'm sure you'd see a word or two.

SPRING

melting snow
finds its
lizard
way
between rock
down
canyon wall
to waiting pool

as the pool overflows
water snakes
to stream
then
as a dragon
joins
the roaring river

SUMMER

the walkingstick chollas
in magenta
salute
the Fourth of July
in fashion

dozens on this prairie
meadow
becoming
a magical forest
where no
forest had been before

AUTUMN

The chilling wind is putting out
Cottonwood flames
Along the stream,
Not all at once,
But leaf by leaf,
Thousands of votive candles
Blown out one by one
In preparation for dark winter.

WINTER

the dark branches of two
cottonwoods
meet to
arch over a distant Pedernal

its flat top the altar
of this outdoor cathedral

twelve small fruit trees
within the arch
stand on a floor of snow

dark branches
upspread
in worship of the sacred

light on the western half
of distant hills
a sign the falling sun

has celebrated another day

SAGEBRUSH

hay fever victims hate it
yellow pollen inducing sneeze and sniffle

Asteraceae
like Snakeweed and Rabbitbrush
for the Sunflower Family

Tridentata
for its three-toothed triangle leaves

Artemisia
for the wife of a famous ruler
in Asia Minor

his name
Mausakas
who died in 353 B.C.

and
for whom
she built a magnificent mausoleum

one of
the Seven Wonders of the Ancient World

from which we get that very word

thought
you'd like to know about the Sagebrush

death is alive

at dawn ghost trees
turn skeleton
along the east ridge
until
pink then yellow
give life
to variant shades of green
and
branches
reach for sustenance

oh!
one tree is dead
it
cries for attention

gets mine—death is alive

CAWS

Yester
morn a little
blackbird
woke me
with its gargle

This
morn four
ravens
are the caws.

I SHALL BASK

Painting of glory these silver rays
through gray-black clouds,

but hint of Homer's blush
and Shakespeare's eye warm on the meadow

cause the clouds to darken, dim the glory.

We will have a somber day.

Yet the bird chirps just as bright,
and the flower searches the unseen sun.

Just so
should we keep the forlorn day.

Not I.

I shall bask in the missing of the sun.

FLOWERBED

This flowerbed is dedicated to
Raymond Martínez
1959-1998
friend to everyone

reads the sign
among the flowers
beside the main portal

friend to everyone

I never knew him
but by looking at the care
the flowers have-

dahlia, gaillardia, geranium
snapdragon, marigold
larkspur, chrysanthemum, and more

orange, blue, yellow, white
red, lavender, pink, and more

shade of green
shape of petal
length of stem

plotted by artist
in brown of ground
in lieu of flowers sent
in sympathy the usual way

friend to everyone

the beauty of this flowerbed
is the image
of Raymond Martínez, I gather

as a flower's image lingers
in the mind
so his image to those who knew him

a friend to everyone

white cliffs of the night

the cliffs of the mesa
celebrate
the full of the moon
reflecting
its shining smile
as if
posing
for
a toothpaste commercial

chenopodiaceae

Chenopodiaceae for the Goosefoot Family
eurotia for its moldy white
lanata for its hairy leaves

tap root deep
side roots
reaching shallow sideways
to water wherever

if the cow could pray
it would thank
God
for this plant in the winter

and people should too
since
they use it as powder for burns
and
a concoction
of its leaves for hay fever

now I wonder what other
plants
belong to *Chenopodiaceae*
and if
they really all look like goosefeet

I've been writing about Winterfat

ROCK IN HEAT OF DAY

A world lives beneath this rock.

One of its creatures just crawled out
to test the heat of the afternoon.
Chin up it eyes
ants
zigzagging
the ground before it,
decides it's too hot to feast,
returns to companions in the cool.

I yearn to overturn the rock
to see the world beneath. Dare I?

morning prayer at Ghost House

as our song in praise
of Creation
fills
this space
beneath the Cottonwoods

I can't help but think
of a brother's
murder
for a pot of gold
of a guest's
murder
for a saddle of silver

this space once Hell

not now

this Heaven moment says so

DENSE NARRATOR

"That's Rubber Rabbitbrush,"
the campground hostess
replied to my question.
Her expansive gesture
included the "Rabbit Xing" sign.

I thought she was trying to twist my tongue.

"Say it fast three times,"
I expected her to add, but she didn't.

I had imagined rubber rabbits,
not rubber brush,

and when she said, "People around here
call it 'chamisa,'"
I remembered articles in the *Daily Tribune*
about planting and harvesting
to make rubber tires
and asked, "Is that idea still adrift?"

She didn't answer
but said,
"*Chryso* for the yellow in the flower,
thamnus for brush, or thicket, or shrub."

My face must have registered
blank
for she instructed,
"It's Latin from the Greek,
and it's *Asteraceae*
because it's related to the Sunflower."

I thought of salted seeds
and wondered if rabbits ate them,
but I didn't ask.

I guess she thought
I was about to ask about *nauseosus*,
for she snapped, "Like English!
It's the smell," and left it at that.

Next morning
on my way to the campground shower,
I saw a rabbit watching me
from a
Chrysothamnus nauseosus Asteraceae.

The smell didn't seem to bother it,
and I wondered
if the Latin
from the Greek
twisted the tongues of Latins and Greeks.

VALLE DE ESPANTOS

Cuando este valle
era el Rancho de los Brujos
espantában
voces
de muertos
lamentando por la noche,
espantában
fantasmas subiendo
por los riscos,
fantasmas de hombres
asesinados
a mano
de los hermanos Archuleta,
fantasmas
moviendo furtivamente
a las orillas
de las fogatas de campamiento,
y
espantában
cuentos
de una víbora por nombre
Vivarón
visto
al puesto del sol
en busca
de niños traviesos.

Tierra maldita
este Rancho de los Brujos.

Hoy día, gracias
a Dios, no
espantan
las fantasmas.

Y
el Vivarón?

Esqueleto
de lagarto gigante

antepasado
imprimido
en piedra que
parece
enroscar,
saltar,
y
serpentear
cuando
sesgan brillando
los rayos
al puesto del sol.

Tierra bendita ahora

con nombre
que parece
ser
del espíritu santo,
este valle
donde vivía el Vivarón.

THIS VALE OF FEARS
(akin to "Valle de Espantos")

this vale
haven of evil
place
where wailing ghosts
elongated
towards the moon
along cliff walls
place
where ghosts were seen
at the campfire's edge
fear of them
felt along the spine
place
where men were murdered
by brothers
one becoming Cain to the other
place
where a frightful snake
haunted
each canyon
hungry for children

cursed place-now no longer cursed

ghosts
no longer seen no longer heard

snake
forgotten when dinosaur bones
were
understood
as a mirage in hillside sand at sunset

place
blessed now
with
name that
seems to praise the Holy Spirit

NARCISO

el correr de la araña
sobre
el charco
arruga mi espejo

viendo mi cara
en tal espejo
me hace
pensar
en los surcos de edad

NARCISSUS
(akin to "Narciso")

the way the water spider
wrinkles
my face
as it darts
across the pool's surface

sets me to thinking
about
Cicero's "De senectute"

timor
mortis conturbat me

crows in winter

       along the Rito del Yeso
       black preying
       leaves
       in a tree
       unlike leaves change trees

at a table near the dining hall

a bee lands on the lip of my rootbeer can

I doff my hat
to chase it but tip the can
spilling sweet liquid upon dry leaves

I reach beneath the table
to retrieve the can
but a dozen bees already crawl
and grapple
over the petal-less nectar

it's as if they had been waiting in hiding

acrophobia

I look down into
this shallow pool mirror
of canyon wall
and sky

so clear

I feel
panic in my hinder parts

a.m. to p.m.

seven
the tall desert rock catches
morning full face

its shadow yawns, stretches west

ten
its shadow disappearing into the rock

noon
its shadow inside asleep

two
its shadow emerging

four
its shadow stretches east

seven
the tall desert rock's turn to sleep

Stopping by Sign 18: Pinyon Pine (Pinus edulis)

Is this the pine that grows piñón,
the pine we spread the sheet beneath and shook
to get nut and cone when I was young?
Looks like it as I remember.
But pinyon (pín-yahn)?
I don't recall that spelling or pronunciation.
Piñón (peenyóhn).
That's what I remember.

Y me acuerdo de mis cousins,
mis tíos, tías, hermanos, hermanas,
abuelo, abuela, mamá, papá, all of us
getting las manos sticky
as we gathered piñón not pinyon.
Pinyon?
Do they roast as well with a name like that?
Ah, the roasting! Aroma from heaven!
And the taste? Aye Dios, delicioso!

Piñón, pinyon, pine nut,
pinyon pine nut, nut pine, and more
appear in dictionaries.

The Colorado National Monument Guide
reads piñón.
A chiropracter's sign reads pinyon.
A recipe in the
Rancho de Chimayo Cookbook reads piñón.
The poetry magazine
at Mesa State College is titled *Pinyon*.

I'm not done.

I looked up *pinus edulis*.
It's Latin
for eatable or edible pine.
Eatable
if you want to flaunt your Anglo-Saxon.
Edible
if you want to flaunt your Latin.

And, oh yes, what we buy at the store
in packages
comes from China.
They're called Pignolia!

All this from stopping
At Sign 18: Pinyon Pine (Pinus edulis). Pinyon?

PIEDRA LUMBRE

       your sunset embers
       glow
       beneath your blue sky

       evening meditation
       glowing
       within my desert soul

ABIQUIU

Take this city-filled
soul,
pour it out,
place it in soil
beneath
your high desert vista.

Fill it with canyon,
sky,
mesa,
mountain,
smell of rain,
and
song of bird.

Tint each
with time of day.

Let each
settle
into a painting of sand

so that when I'm away
I can
close my eyes
and gaze upon
and breathe your sacred strands.